Everything Democrats know about Life, Success, and Happiness in America

Dr. I. M. Astatist, Ph.D.

ISBN: 0975465619
ISBN-13: 978-0-9754656-1-5

DEDICATION

To Life, Success, and Happiness in America

Everything Democrats know about Life, Success, and Happiness in America

Dr. I. M. Astatist

Everything Democrats know about Life, Success, and Happiness in America

Dr. I. M. Astatist

Everything Democrats know about Life, Success, and Happiness in America

Dr. I. M. Astatist

Everything Democrats know about Life, Success, and Happiness in America

Dr. I. M. Astatist

Dr. I. M. Astatist

Dr. I. M. Astatist

Everything Democrats know about Life, Success, and Happiness in America

Dr. I. M. Astatist

Everything Democrats know about Life, Success, and Happiness in America

Dr. I. M. Astatist

Everything Democrats know about Life, Success, and Happiness in America

Dr. I. M. Astatist

Dr. I. M. Astatist

Everything Democrats know about Life, Success, and Happiness in America

Dr. I. M. Astatist

Everything Democrats know about Life, Success, and Happiness in America

Dr. I. M. Astatist

Everything Democrats know about Life, Success, and Happiness in America

Dr. I. M. Astatist

Dr. I. M. Astatist

Dr. I. M. Astatist

Dr. I. M. Astatist

Everything Democrats know about Life, Success, and Happiness in America

Dr. I. M. Astatist

Dr. I. M. Astatist

Dr. I. M. Astatist

Dr. I. M. Astatist

Dr. I. M. Astatist

Dr. I. M. Astatist

Dr. I. M. Astatist

Dr. I. M. Astatist

Dr. I. M. Astatist

Dr. I. M. Astatist

Dr. I. M. Astatist

Everything Democrats know about Life, Success, and Happiness in America

Dr. I. M. Astatist

Dr. I. M. Astatist

Dr. I. M. Astatist

Dr. I. M. Astatist

Everything Democrats know about Life, Success, and Happiness in America

Dr. I. M. Astatist

Everything Democrats know about Life, Success, and Happiness in America

Dr. I. M. Astatist

Everything Democrats know about Life, Success, and Happiness in America

Dr. I. M. Astatist

Dr. I. M. Astatist

Everything Democrats know about Life, Success, and Happiness in America

Everything Democrats know about Life, Success, and Happiness in America

Dr. I. M. Astatist

Everything Democrats know about Life, Success, and Happiness in America

Dr. I. M. Astatist

Dr. I. M. Astatist

Dr. I. M. Astatist

Dr. I. M. Astatist

Everything Democrats know about Life, Success, and Happiness in America

Dr. I. M. Astatist

Dr. I. M. Astatist

Dr. I. M. Astatist

Everything Democrats know about Life, Success, and Happiness in America

Dr. I. M. Astatist

Dr. I. M. Astatist

Dr. I. M. Astatist

Dr. I. M. Astatist

Dr. I. M. Astatist

Everything Democrats know about Life, Success, and Happiness in America

Dr. I. M. Astatist

Dr. I. M. Astatist

Dr. I. M. Astatist

ABOUT THE AUTHOR

Dr. I. M. Astatist is an accomplished author and academic as well as an enthusiastic supporter of the Democrat party. He studied abroad for several years and considers himself a citizen of the world. He finally settled down to write and teach environmental and social studies at the university level. He is a tireless advocate for animal rights, green energy, social equality and increased government oversight of the free market.